A panorama of Tallinn

TALLINN

Tallinn, the capital of the Republic of Estonia, a small, but unusually beautiful medieval city on the Eastern shore of the Baltic Sea.

Throughout its stormy history, despite the changing foreign rulers, wars, fires and reconstruction, the city has nevertheless retained its beauty and integrity untouched, maintaining its medieval environment and atmosphere. In fact, one of the main values of Tallinn is that a large share of the old buildings have preserved almost undamaged, which turns it into one of the best-preserved medieval trading towns in the whole Europe. Thanks to this Tallinn has been entered in the UN list of world heritage as a real living museum and a fine example of the heyday of the Hansatic League trading towns.

The present Tallinn area was first inhabited approximately in the end of the 10th century, when the Estonian tribes built a stronghold on the Toompea hill, in the immediate vicinity of the port, thanks to its advantageous location near to the sea and the position at the East-West trading route. The famous Arab explorer al-Idrisi market Tallinn on his world map as early as in 1154, commenting: "Koluvan is a small town with a large stronghold." The town was known under different names at that time: the Slavs called it Koluvan and the Scandinavians Lindanise. The buildings of that period were wooden and have not survived.

A view of Tallinn old town

Crusaders led by King Valdemar II of Denmark conquered the Tallinn stronghold in 1219, built their own fortress there and began the seven hundred year period, during which the town was ruled by foreigners. The official name of the town until the beginning of the

1

A bird's eye view of Tallinn

20th century was Reval.

A number of merchants from Gotland, an important trade centre of that time, settled in Tallinn in the 1230s. This event is considered significant in the forming of the early Tallinn citizenry. Thus the Reval of that time belonged to the German-language towns and German language and culture dominated here until the first decades of the 20th century.

King Erik Plogpenning of Denmark granted the Lübeck bylaws in 1248, reflecting the moral standards and mentality of these times, which were used to organise the affairs of the town. The municipal self-government - the town council - was also mentioned for the first time in 1248.

Medieval Tallinn turned into one of the largest and most powerful trading towns of Northern Europe with densely-built stone houses, thanks to the trading routes of the other Western European Hanseatic towns and the Russian territories passing through it.

A view of the port

Panorama of Tallinn at sunset

Tallinn joined the Hanseatic league of the German trading towns in the 13th century.

The medieval Tallinn has been built of local limestone, the use of this material resulting in a very heavy and massive Gothic style.

The Tallinn old town consists of two parts:

Toompea - located on a limestone elevation 20-30 metres above the rest of the town. This area belonged to the representatives of the nobility and the state power since the 13th century and was set apart of the downtown, both administratively and by a protective wall;

the downtown - located between Toompea and the seaport, governed according to the Lübeck town bylaws, a member of the Hanseatic League and populated by free burghers, who were governed by the town council. The downtown was surrounded by a wall;

Outside the town wall were the belt of protective earthworks and the water-filled moat, as well as several suburbs, which unfortunately were frequently destroyed in wars.

Tallinn presents an unusual and attractive seaside silhouette with the high Toompea, where the Estonian national flag flies, the pointed church spires and red roofs of the houses and towers of the town wall.

A view of Toompea

TOOMPEA

The tower of Tall Hermann

A beautiful legend from the Estonian national epic "Kalevipoeg" tells us about Linda, the wife of the ancient Estonian hero Kalev, who carried stones in her apron to Toompea to build her dead husband's grave mound. The weary Linda, carrying the last stone, sat down on the grave and cried. Her tears formed the Lake Ülemiste near Tallinn and Toompea is still sometimes referred to as Kalev's grave.

Another legend about the lake of tears itself tells that a small grey old man comes every autumn on midnight to the guards of the town gate, asking whether Tallinn has been completed. As soon as the building town has been completed, he will release the waters of the lake and flood Tallinn.

Since Toompea is located on a hill, the ancient Estonian built a wooden stronghold here as early as in the 11th century, when the first settlers arrived there. The foreign rulers replaced it by a stone fortress. As Toompea has been ravaged by a number of large fires in 1288, 1433, 1553, 1684, the earlier buildings have been largely lost. The present fortress dates back to the 14th-15th centuries.

Toompea Castle, western side

Façade of Toompea Castle

Toompea has been the seat of the higher local representatives of the state and religious authorities through the ages and still retains the tradition - Toompea palace houses the parliament of the Republic of Estonia. The Estonian national flag flies over the highest tower of the Toompea castle - the 50-metre Tall Hermann.

The Government of the Republic of Estonia and the office of the prime minister are also located in Toompea in Stenbock House. This is a beautiful Classicist building over a high limestone cliff, which has been rebuilt to house the government.

German Embassy building in Toompea

THE VIEWING TERRACES OF TOOMPEA

Kohtuotsa viewing terrace

A view of the city from Kohtuotsa terrace

Toompea provides a number of fine opportunities to enjoy the wonderful view from the high hill. There are several viewing terraces in Toompea, the largest and best-known of which are the Kohtuotsa and Patkul terraces. These platforms give pleasant and memorable opportunities to have a bird's-eye view of Tallinn all year round.

The Kohtuotsa terrace opens a beautiful view towards the Town Hall and directly down to the Long Leg Street and its gate tower. The spire of the Holy Ghost Church and the dense medieval streets with red tile gable roofs can be seen nearby.

The Patkul terrace is in the immediate vicinity of Stenbock House, the seat of the Government of Estonia and the prime minister's office. The Patkul terrace provides a romantic and impressive view towards the sea and the port. In a clear day one can see the Tallinn waterfront as far as the sight can reach. As for the

Patkul Stairs and Stenbock House (residence of the Government) in Toompea

Patkul viewing terrace

old town sights, the pointed red-roofed towers of the town wall can be seen up close, while further away is the St. Olav's Church with its skywards-stretching spire - the highest building in the old town - and there are of course the narrow cobblestone streets.

A zigzag staircase along the limestone cliff descends from the Patkul terrace. It leads to a park to the west of Toompea, which separates the old town from the new districts and is the site of the Snell Pond, the only surviving stretch of the old protective moat.

A view of the city from Patkul terrace

The Snell pond

Stenbock House (residence of the Government) in Toompea

THE DOME CHURCH

A wooden church was built in Toompea as early as in 1219. Monks of the Dominican Order started the construction of a stone church in 1229. A bloody conflict took place in Toompea in 1233 between the two camps of the crusaders - the Danish forces and the German order of the Brethren of the Sword, which allegedly carried over into the church. Toompea has suffered from numerous major fires as well as from the wars. The 1684 fire destroyed nearly all the buildings in Toompea as well as the church. Although the church was restored to its previous shape, much of the interior dates back to later periods. The Baroque spire of the church dates back to 1779. The church's unique collection of more than 100 coats-of-arms of Baltic German noblemen is worth noting. Grave markers from the

The Cathedral of Saint Mary the Virgin (Dome Church)

Organ pipes in the Cathedral of Saint Mary the Virgin

The cathedral organ

9

The pulpit of the cathedral and noblemen's coats of arms on the wall

Interior view of the cathedral

13th-18th centuries and sarcophagi of the 17th century can also be seen. The beautifully carved altar and pulpit and the chandeliers date back to the 17th century. The organ made by the famous organ builder Fr. Landegast in 1878 is another object of pride in of the church. The church has four bells, two cast in the 17th and two in the 18th century.

Altar of the cathedral

Interior view of the cathedral

Night view of the Cathedral of Saint Mary the Virgin

ALEXANDER NEVSKY CATHEDRAL

Patriarch Alexi II of Moscow and Russia

Christianity reached Estonia simultaneously from the West and the East, Catholicism from the West and the Russian Orthodox faith from the East. There is reliable evidence that a Russian church existed in Tallinn in the 13th century. It is quite likely that it was founded even earlier. The present St. Nickolas` Church in Vene (Russian) Street can be considered the successor of the first Russian church.

The construction of the Alexander Nevsky Cathedral took place during the rule of the Russian Czars Alexander III and Nicholas II in the end of the 19th century under the supervision of Prince Shakhovskoi, the governor of Estonia.

An all-Russian collection of money was organised for the construction of the cathedral. It was decided to build it in Toompea, where it could dominate the silhouette of the city. The design of the church is by the St. Petersburg Academy of Arts member M.

Iconostasis of the Alexander Nevsky Cathedral

Alexander Nevsky Cathedral

Icon of the All-holy Theotokos "Painstaking Lay Sister"

Interior view of the Alexander Nevsky Cathedral

Preobrazhensky. The cathedral was built in the traditional style of old Russian churches. The completed building with five bulbous spires represents a later stage of the Russian Historicist style. The façade is richly decorated with mosaic panels by A. Frolov, which are unique in Estonia's architecture as to their size and masterful execution. Academician Preobrazhensky's designs were also used for the three wooden iconostases and four icon cupboards in the

Christmas celebration in the Alexander Nevsky Cathedral

church. The icons were painted by A. Novoskoltsev. A characteristic feature of the Russian Orthodox is the great attention paid to the bell ringing. The bells cast in St. Petersburg weigh a total of 27 tons, the weight of the main bell being 16 tons.

The cathedral was consecrated in 1900 by Archbishop Agafangel of Riga and Mitav. The Alexander Nevsky Cathedral has a special status - it is directly subordinated to the patriarch of Moscow and Russia.

Winter view of the Alexander Nevsky Cathedral

THE LONG LEG AND THE SHORT LEG

The Long Leg and the Short Leg are two streets, which start from the same point and connect Toompea with the downtown. The Long Leg is much wider and could be travelled by carriages and coaches. The other street - the Short Leg - was meant only for pedestrians and it is rather steep.

The Long Leg Street

The Long Leg gate tower was built in 1380 as a three-story building with the portal and portcullis being to the Toompea side of the tower. The stretch of wall separating Toompea from the downtown was built at the same time, because relations between the two were not always cordial. On the contrary, the two centres of power were constantly in conflict and the gates of the Long and Short legs were closed every night, cutting off all traffic between the two parts of the town. This is why the stretch of wall got the popular name of Feud Wall. The tower was rebuilt in the 1450s,

View of the Long Leg gate tower from Toompea

Gate tower of the Long Leg

adding two more stories, the three upper levels being fortified and the two others housing the mechanisms of the portcullis.

It is believed that the Short Leg was built as early as in the 1230s to link the settlement of German merchants in the downtown to Toompea.

The Short Leg gate tower was built in 1454-56 at the border between the two parts of the town in the upper end of the street, where it also joins the Short Leg with the Long Leg. The four-story tower was rhomboid in plan. The arched passageway was on the ground floor and included two portals with massive doors; one of the doors with nails forged in the 17th century has been preserved. The tower was also fitted with a portcullis.

Danish King's Garden. Monument to the flag of Denmark

Next to the Short Leg Tower is the Danish King's Garden. According to a legend, a red flag with a white cross fell from the sky in a battle for Tallinn in 1219, when the Estonians were overcoming the Danes; this miracle encouraged the Danes to win the battle. A stone marks the place of the event in the Danish King's Garden. The white cross on red background became the Danish national flag as well as the Tallinn coat of arms.

Danish King's Garden

The Short Leg Street

16

THE ST. NICHOLAS CHURCH

St. Nicholas`church (Niguliste) was most probably founded in the middle of the 13th century, and dedicated to St. Nicholas, the patron saint of the merchants and seafarers. The church acquired its present appearance in the course of different periods of style, form early Gothic till the 19th century. It is one of the most remarkable medieval church buildings in Tallinn and in the whole architectural heritage of Estonia.

The building was active as a church until World War II. After the fire on 9 March 1944 the building was reconstructed and adjusted to the needs of a museum and a concert hall. In 1984 it was opened to the public as a branch of the Art Museum of Estonia. In the Niguliste Museum, one can mainly admire medieval church art but also objects from the Renaissance and the Baroque. Several works of art that have historically belonged to St. Nicholas`church have made their way back there, above all the world-famous initial

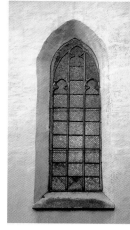

Stained glass window of St. Nicholas Church (Niguliste)

Door portal of St. Nicholas Church (Niguliste)

St. Nicholas Church (Niguliste)

*"Dance Macabre"
by Bernt Notke*

*Main altar of St.
Nicholas Church.
Hermen Rode*

fragment of the *Dance Macabre* by Bernt Notke (late 15th c.) and the magnificent high altar by Hermen Rode (1478-1481). The exposition also contains other altarpieces of high value: the *Altar of St. Mary* (made by an author of "The Legend of St. Lucy", late 15th c.), and the Altar of Christ`s Passion (the workshop of Adriaen Isenbrandt?, ca. 1515). A panel painting from the late Middle Ages (a master from the Palace of Lichtenstein *"Presentation of Christ*

18

in the Temple", ca. 1430-1440) and several medieval polychrome woodcarvings (*St. Nicholas, Virgin Mary, John the Evangelist*, ca. 1510-1520) are represented in the collection. The exposition contains fragments of pews (16-17th c.), the figure of St. Christopher (Tobias Heintze, 1624), the memorial stone of Antonius van der Busch (Arent Passer, ca. 1608), and tombstones and their fragments (14-17th c.). Noteworthy are numerous epitaphs and coats-of-arms (17-18th c.), the grand seven-armed candelabrum (1519), and several chandeliers and sconces (16-18th c.).

The Silver Chamber of the museum has been open to the public since November 2001. This exhibition consists of three parts: church silver, guild silver, and silver of the Brotherhood of the Black Heads in Tallinn. The oldest treasures originate from the 15th century, the youngest from the beginning of the 20th century. The Niguliste Museum offers guided tours, and there is a tradition of celebrating the feast days of St. Nicholas (6 December and 9 may).

Half-hour organ music concerts take place on Saturdays and Sundays. The organ was built in 1981 by the Rieger-Kloss Company and has 4 manuals, a pedal, 63 registers, and 4711 pipes. The Niguliste Museum - Concert Hall is also known as a venue of the Tallinn International Organ festivals.

Interior view of St. Nicholas Church

19

St Nicholas Church (Niguliste)

The Wheel Well and Dunkri Street

Rataskaevu Street

Rataskaevu Square and the Wheel Well

Water supply is not a modern problem, it was an important matter in the Middle Ages as well. The Tallinn town council documents first mentioned the town well, currently known as the Wheel Well, in 1357. The actual name dates back to a more recent past - when it was fitted with a wheel for easier lifting of heavy buckets with water.

Town Hall in the Christmas season

Town Hall weather vanes

THE TOWN HALL

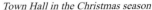

Baroque gargoyle of the Town Hall

Old Thomas weather vane

The Town Hall located along the southern side of the Town Hall Square was a representative building of the medieval Tallinn, which also housed the government of the town. According to the Lübeck town bylaws, Tallinn was a town governed by the council, elected from among members of the Great Guild. The town council was responsible for the management of the town and decided all issues concerning its affairs.

For example, the competence of the Tallinn town council covered the approval of dress code, which meant restrictions imposed on the clothing of the burghers' wives. However, this allegedly caused protests among the wives of the aldermen, who complained that the council's tastes were too old-fashioned.

The Tallinn Town Hall was first built in 1322, but its present size and shape date back to 1402-04. It is also one of the few Gothic town halls in Northern Europe to have preserved its original style.

As seen towards the main façade, the building rests on an open arcade of ogival arches, while the windows are rectangular. On the other hand, the rear façade features simpler ogival arch windows. A high, eight-sided tower rises over the eastern gable, bearing a Baroque spire built in 1627-28. Its top is decorated by the soldier-shaped weathervane Old Thomas, which has become one of the symbols of the Tallinn old town. At the same time, the main façade was fitted with dragon-shaped gargoyles and two small shops with

The Citizens' Hall   *The Council Hall*

Baroque roofs were built along the western side. The first Old Thomas was placed in the spire in 1530. The present one is the third in service. The first figure ended its more than 400 year service after a bomb hit in 1944, the second one lasted more than 40 years and the third started in 1996.

The rooms of all three storeys of the Town Hall have arched ceilings. The building was fitted with all necessary facilities for the magistrate's needs. The storage rooms were in the cellar, the ground floor housed the torture chamber, the large goods hall, the treasury and the other household areas. The main storey was very ornate as it housed the most important and ceremonial rooms of the Town Hall: the large two-nave citizens' hall used for parties and receptions and the town council hall, where the aldermen held court, receptions and sessions.

The Town Hall is still used as a representative building of the city government. It is used for ceremonial receptions, concerts and exhibitions.

A view of the Town Hall basement

Town Hall Square

TOWN HALL SQUARE

Old town festival

The Town Hall Square became a centre of the Tallinn downtown and the main square as early as in the 13th century as an Estonian settlement was developing around it. The market place was first mentioned in written sources in 1313. The market was the centre of Tallinn and enjoyed special significance. A number of small shops were built around it. There used to be a well in the centre of the square. Most of the streets leading to the square were defined in 1402-04 and have survived until our days.

All main meetings, parties and receptions were held in the Town Hall Square. The square was also the site of tournaments and the working place of the executioner, where those guilty of minor crimes received punishment. The neck irons and handcuffs of the pillory are still shown on one of the pillars of the Town hall arcade. Executions were held outside the town limits on Hanging Hill.

Christmas trees have been set up in the Town Hall Square for centuries. A chronicle from the 16th century describes the

Town Hall Square

Medieval market in Town Hall Square

Medieval market in Town Hall Square and celebration of the old town festival

*Town Hall
Pharmacy*

*Forged
decoration on
Town Hall
Pharmacy wall*

*Medieval building
in Town Hall
Square*

tradition to burn the Christmas trees in the square and the accompanying drinking and disorderly conduct around the fire.

The Town Hall Square is still a place for all kinds of events, which are frequently organised there. The most extensive event is the old town festival held every summer, which includes concerts and a fair of handicraft, also described as a medieval market.

Several other important buildings were constructed around the Town Hall. The town council prison was built in the narrow street behind the Town Hall. It is presently used as the Town Hall Museum.

Another important building is the Town Hall Pharmacy, which can be seen in the north-eastern part of the square next to the round gateway of the Saiakang passage – a narrow walkway leading to Pikk (Long) Street, the Church of Holy Ghost and the building of the Great Guild. The Saiakang passageway was then lined by small shops. The Town Hall Pharmacy was first mentioned in records in 1422, when the apothecary Niclawes attended a town council session, but it is likely that drugs were sold in the same place even earlier. The Burchart dynasty of apothecaries started in the pharmacy in the end of the 16th century and lasted for 300 years, through ten generations. A medieval pharmacy was an important trading place, which was not limited to drugs – it also sold wine, textile, paper, gunpowder and shot, wax, spices, sweets etc. Pharmacies of that time also sold precious stones, either intact or powdered. For example, the Town Hall Pharmacy could offer beryl against jaundice, sapphire against bubonic plague and amethyst to cure from drinking.

Town Hall Pharmacy

Views of Saiakang passage, the Holy Ghost Church in the background

27

A view of the Holy Ghost Church and clock of the Holy Ghost Church

CHURCH OF THE HOLY GHOST

The Church of the Holy Ghost was probably built, together with the Holy Ghost Almshouse, in the first half of the 13th century. It is possible that the tradition extends even further into the past, since the local Estonians were reported to have had a chapel near the Town Hall Square before the Danish conquest. The present two-nave shape dates back to the 14th century. The late Renaissance style spire was built in 1688.

The Holy Ghost Church

The bell of the church - the Mary Bell - was cast in 1433 and survived until 2002, when it was lost in a fire. The church façade clock with Baroque wooden carvings, made by Christian Ackermann, is the oldest public timepiece in Tallinn.

The church has a rich collection of art treasures. The most important is the cupboard altar made by Bernt Notke in 1483. Other notable sights are the 1597 pulpit with Renaissance carvings, the painted and carved 16th-17th century choir lofts and banisters, numerous chandeliers of the same period and the benches made in the 16th-19th centuries.

Since the Church of the Holy Ghost had an Estonian congregation, it has close ties with the Estonian cultural history. S. Wanradt and J. Koell, the compilers of the first Estonian-language catechism, the oldest surviving Estonian-language printed book (1535), worked here. Balthasar Russow, the chronicler, who wrote the "Livonian Chronicle" containing important data about Estonian history, worked here in 1563-1600, while Georg Müller, who recorded 39 Estonian-language texts, was the pastor of the church in 1601-1608.

PIKK STREET AND THE GUILD HOUSES

The House of the Great Guild

Pikk Street (Long Street) is the longest street of the old town, leading from Toompea to the port. It used to be the main street of the town, where the most important public buildings were located, for example, the houses of the guilds, which joined the representatives of various professions.

The former house of the Great Guild stands in 17 Pikk Street, immediately opposite the Church of Holy Ghost. The first records of the guild date back to 1325, but the building was completed in 1410. Only the most wealthy and respected residents of the town could be admitted to the Guild - major merchants, who also had to be married and citizens of Tallinn. All the more important officials of the town - including the aldermen - were elected only from among the members of the Great Guild. The Guild's coat of arms is the small coat of arms of Tallinn - white cross on red field. The House of the Great Guild and its large hall with groined arches, supported by three pillars, was often used for major celebrations, weddings and receptions of important guests. The building presently houses the Estonian History Museum.

The House of the Kanut Guild is located in 20 Pikk Street. The Kanut Guild joined skilled German handicraftsmen, e.g. goldsmiths, watchmakers, shoemakers, glovemakers, bakers, etc. The building was extensively rebuilt in the Tudor style in the 1860s. The figures of Martin Luther and St. Kanut were placed in the façade.

It is thought that the St. Olav Guild (house located in 24

The House of the Kanut Guild and door portal of the Great Guild Hall

The House of the St. Olav's (Oleviste) Guild

Pikk Street) was founded even before the Kanut Guild. This guild joined non-German, including Estonian, representatives of the less skilled specialities. The guild house has been repeatedly reconstructed during past centuries, but the arched hall, dating back to 1422, has been retained.

The house of the Brotherhood of the Black Heads in 26 Pikk Street is nearly the sole surviving renaissance building in Tallinn. The Brotherhood was formed in 1399 and was an organisation of unmarried merchants, concentrating on the protection of their interests and organisation of social affairs. The name of the organisation refers to their patron saint, the African St. Mauritius, who was executed for his adoption of the Christian faith. The brotherhood moved to the present location in 1531, when the construction began, and Arendt Passer completed the beautiful Renaissance façade with its numerous decorations in 1597. The coat of arms of the Black Heads, which depicts St. Mauritius, is mounted over the portal.

The coat of arms of the Brotherhood of Blackheads

House of the Brotherhood of Blackheads, The House of St. Olav's Guild

30

A view of Pikk Street

THE THREE SISTERS

*Façade of
a medieval
merchant's house*

The complex of medieval residential buildings, known as the Three Sisters, is at the end of Pikk Street (71 Pikk Str.) near the Great Coastal Gate, and consists of three adjacent buildings, each with a separate gable roof. The group of buildings dates back to the 15th century. The Three Sisters is a typical medieval merchant's home, which consisted of an entrance hall, a small chimney kitchen, the master's office and living and sleeping chambers. Store rooms were placed above the living quarters. Beams used to hoist goods to the storerooms can still be seen at the top of the gables. The ceiling beams were accordingly massive and placed close to each other. The building naturally included a cellar, a store and a back yard with the servants' quarters, beer cellar, stables and other necessary buildings.

Some reconstruction was made in the 19th century, but the upper facades of all three buildings have remained unchanged. The oldest of the three buildings is the largest one to the south, which dates back to 1415. This is also the building to have retained the most of its original appearance. It has a remarkable staircase and the façade is decorated with rounded recesses. There are three hatches for the loading of goods. The ornate Baroque door of 1651 has been preserved as well.

Views of the "Three Sisters"

ST. OLAV`S CHURCH

The St. Olav's Church was Tallinn's most impressive building in the Middle Ages and belonged to the tallest buildings of the world. Although written records mention the church since 1267, it is thought that it already existed in the same place in the 12th century as a centre of a Scandinavian market place.

The church was actually built in several stages during the later centuries. It reached its present size and shape in the 15th century and was named after King Olav II Haraldson of Norway, who was canonised. A beautiful choir room with stellar vaults was built then and has retained its original appearance. The St. Mary's Chapel was built in 1512-21 and a magnificent example of stone carving, the Hans Pawels cenotaph, is located in it outer wall. The church's Gothic steeple was built in the 15th -16th centuries and its immense height, 159 metres, made it the world's tallest building for some time. The steeple was also used as a navigational sign, announcing the trading town's location to seafarers from a great distance. Unfortunately, the height of the steeple also involved the risk of attracting lightning during thunderstorms and resulted in devastating fires. Lightning hit the steeple in 1651 and in 1820, causing major damage to the entire

St. Olav's Church

Views of the St. Olav's Church central nave and altar

Views of the organ of St. Olav's Church

church. Nearly the whole interior was lost in the fire and some vaults collapsed as well. The restoration lasted 20 years under the supervision of the art historian F. Maydell, who favoured the use of neo-Gothic style in the repair. Thus most of the exterior details of the church date back to the 15th century with added neo-Gothic elements. The present steeple is also 36 metres lower than the original and only rises to 123 metres.

According to a legend, the church received its name after the master builder. The town had decided to build a tall church, which could be seen far on the sea, but lacked money for the effort. A mysterious building master offered his help, promising to build the church free of charge if someone should guess his name. Otherwise he would state the fee himself. As the master was placing the cross to the top of the steeple, someone called his name. The startled builder, named Olev, lost his grip and fell to his death. Accordingly, the church was named Oleviste to commemorate him.

St. Mary's Chapel, The Hans Pawels cenotaph in the outer wall of St. Mary's Chapel

St. Olav's Church

35

LAI (BROAD) STREET, THE THREE BROTHERS

View of Lai Street

Lai Street is notable for several significant medieval burgher's houses, which have preserved very well. These are the buildings in 23, 29 and 40 Lai Street, also known as the Three Brothers.

23 Lai Street, the current building of the City Theatre, dates back to the 14th - 15th centuries and was initially used as a residence with the living rooms on the ground floor and the storage rooms in the attic. A staircase decorated with the family coat of arms leads to the main entrance. The staircase was also used to hoist goods to the storage rooms. The entrance staircases of most Tallinn buildings were demolished in the beginning of the 19th century, when the governor's coach got stuck against one and was overturned.

The house in 29 Lai Street, known as the Hueck house, dates back to the same period as the present City Theatre building. Two ancient lindens grow in front of the building and legends claim that they were planted by the Russian Czar Peter the Great. Another legend claims that the drunken Czar had fallen asleep between the two lindens. The only certain fact is that Czar Peter once visited the Hueck house.

The house in 23 Lai Street

The building in 40 Lai Street is the central house of the Three Brothers. Its current size and shape date back to the 15th century and its medieval constructions are still unusually well preserved. Typical of the medieval residential houses, it consisted of a two-part entrance hall and living quarters on the ground floor and storage rooms upstairs.

In the end of Lai Street, near to the town wall, there is a small round building of 16 metre diameter, known as the Horse Mill. It was built in the first half of the 14th century and its function was to grind flour in case there should be problems with the watermills or during sieges.

The Horse Mill

A view of the Dominican Monastery courtyard

Courtyard and the St. Peter and Paul Church

THE DOMINICAN MONASTERY

The Dominicans arrived in Tallinn in 1229 and initially founded their monastery in Toompea. They had to leave there after a while due to conflicts with the German knights. The Dominican monks founded the monastery again in 1246 in downtown in a plot between the Vene and Müürivahe streets. The building continued with varying success until the beginning of the 16th century and multi-storeyed buildings were erected around a square courtyard. The St. Catherine's Church at the monastery was also completed in the 15th century, as well as a cloister.

The Dominican Monastery played an important part in promoting education in Estonia. Some of the monks learned Estonian and advanced the written Estonian.

The activities of the monastery ended in 1525 with the Lutheran Reformation, which led to the confiscation of the monastery's property and the expulsion of the monks. The monastery church was destroyed in a fire six years later and most of the buildings were ruined in the course of time.

The remaining parts of the building complex are part of the church walls, the cloister, the chapter hall, the sacristy and some rooms of the eastern wing.

West cloister

A view of Vene Street

THE LATIN QUARTER

The Latin Quarter is a term used about the Dominican Monastery and the adjacent buildings in Vene Street. It symbolises an effort to preserve and maintain medieval spirituality. Some remarkable buildings are also located in Vene Street.

In the immediate vicinity of the Dominican monastery there are two churches. The first - the neo-Gothic St. Peter and St. Paul Catholic church, was built at the site of the former refectory of the Dominican monastery and consecrated in 1845. Some reconstruction was done later and the present façade of the church dates back to 1920.

The second church - the St. Nickolas the Miracle Worker Orthodox Church - is the first Classicist church building in Tallinn, with a characteristic domed roof and two rectangular towers with cupolas. The predecessor of the present church was the centre of the Russian market place, which was presumably built in the 11th century in the site of the present-day Sulevimägi. The church burned down in the fire of 1433. According to the

St. Nickolas the Miracle Worker Church in Vene Street

Altar of the St. Nickolas the Miracle Worker Church

A view of Vene Street

St. Peter and Paul Catholic Church

Pskov chronicles, the whole of Tallinn burned down - „burned together with all its churches, houses and organs ". The church was restored in its current location in Vene Street. The previous building was demolished in the 1820s and the present one built.

A narrow archway leads from Vene Street to the St. Catherine's Passage (Katariina käik), which is considered one of the most romantic places in Tallinn. The St. Catherine's Passage runs along the southern wall of the St. Catherine's Church, remnant of the Dominican monastery. It has turned into a favourite place among the tourists due to a large number of interesting handicrafts workshops and arts galleries, where the visitors can observe the craftsmen at work. A small romantic café allows one simply to enjoy the medieval atmosphere.

Entry to the Catherine Passage

Views of the Catherine Passage

Tallinn City Museum

Medieval kitchen

THE TALLINN TOWN MUSEUM

The Tallinn Town Museum is located in a recently renovated medival merchant`s house in the heart of the town. The history of the building dates back to the 14th century, it belonged for centuries to important citizens of Tallinn - merchants and town councilmen. The museum has been here since 1965.

The new permanent exhibition "The city, which will be never complete" is an attractive and modern display of the city`s history, from the beginning up to nowadays. The exhibition uses background sound, mannequins, original articles, videos and old documentaries.

Door portal of the City Museum

A selection of exhibits of the City Museum

VIRU STREET

The network of streets of Tallinn downtown is rather old, a result of consistent development. The old town may look like a disorderly labyrinth at first glance, but the origin of the Tallinn streets is actually quite logical and rational as they linked the most important components of the town - the port, the stronghold, the market place, the towers and the residential districts. The surviving medieval network of streets is a sight in its own rights.

Only a short distance away from the Town Hall is a junction of three streets - the Vana turu kael or Old Market Place. This was the town market place centuries ago. The Kuninga (King) Street leading to Toompea, the Vene (Russian) Street leading to the port and the Suur-Karja and Viru streets leading to the town gates all start here. Viru Street ends with the Viru Gate.

The Viru Gate was first built in the mid-14th century, but they have been constantly rebuilt during the past centuries. The medieval Tallinn gates were all well fortified, consisting of one or more foregates and the square main gate. In order to permit entry, a drawbridge was lowered over a moat filled

Viru Gate

Viru Gate

A view of Viru Street

A section of Viru Gate

with water. The medieval Tallinn had six gates, but only two have survived by now: the Viru Gate and the Great Coastal Gate

Out of the Viru Gate the foregate towers, dating back to the 15th century, and auxiliary buildings, constructed in the 19th century, have survived. The main gate was situated slightly to the rear, in line with the town wall and a covered passageway connected it with the foregate. A dammed pond was dug in front of the gates in the 15th century and the earthworks were renovated. The Viru Gate was closed down in the 17th century due to the construction of bastions and passage through the gates was reopened only in the second half of the 19th century , when the bastions were dismantled.

The present Viru Street has become favourite spot among the tourists as it leads one from the heart of the modern city straight to the centre of the old town - the Town Hall Square. The cobblestone street is also surrounded by beautiful buildings housing many small shops, cafes and restaurants. Most of the buildings date back to the recent centuries, but several well-preserved medieval buildings can be seen in the end of the street around the old market place.

Old market place

Warehouse and Town Hall

A view of Viru Street

43

THE TALLINN TOWN WALL

The Towers Square. Back-of-the-Grusbeke, Epping, Plate and Kõismäe towers

The downtown Tallinn was protected by a wall as early as in the 13th century, but the fence was most probably wooden. More extensive fortification of the town began approximately from 1310, when the walled-in area was extended and the building of a stone wall began. The town wall developed steadily, dependent on the growth and spreading of the town, and its definite shape was reached by the mid-16th century after a nearly 300-year construction process. Tallinn also became one of the best fortified towns in Northern Europe.

The town wall in the middle of the 16th century was 2.5 kilometres long, up to three metres thick with a height of nearly 16 metres. There were 35 towers, including eight gate towers - two inner gates for connection with Toompea and six outer gates. The defensive systems of the latter included 11 advance towers and foregates. The wall was double in the most important places.

Together with the introduction of firearms it became apparent in the 15th century that the wall alone will not ensure reliable defence. An extensive construction of earthworks and a moat began in the second half of the 16th century. The heyday of the

Aerial view of the town wall

Maiden Tower (Neitsitorn), Kiek in de Kök

Loewenschede Tower,
Back-of-the-nuns Tower

Maiden Tower

Kiek in de Kök

Sauna Tower and Kuldjala Tower

Müürivahe Street, Hellemann Tower

A section of the town wall

earthen fortifications - bastions - lasted until the beginning of the 18-19 centuries, when they were mostly flattened and the moat filled up. The only surviving stretch of the old moat is situated along the western slope of Toompea and is known as the Snell Pond.

The part of the town wall survived until the present day is 1.85 kilometres long and includes 25 gate and wall towers. The best-preserved stretch of the wall runs along the Towers Square, where the defensive gallery has been restored between the Nunne, Sauna and Kuldjala towers.

Tallinn's second surviving foregate - the Great Coastal Gate - is located in the town wall at the end of Lai Street and opens to the port. The gate was initially built in the middle of the 14th century, but it has been periodically reconstructed and fortified, including the construction of the foregate in front of the main gate. The foregate was thoroughly reconstructed in the first half

Stolting Tower and Fat Margaret Tower

Foregate of the Great Coastal Gate

Dolomite coat of arms to the left, marked the completion of the tower in the 16ᵗʰ century. The Fat Margaret Tower and Stolting Tower to the right.

of the 16th century with a slender gate tower being built to one side of the gate and a gun tower of 25 metre diameter, dubbed Paks Margareeta (Fat Margaret) The small carved coat of arms of Tallinn was fixed to the wall after the completion of the work and it can still be seen there. The Fat Margaret tower is one of the most remarkable fortified towers besides Tall Hermann and Kiek in de Kök. The walls of the tower are 6,5 metres thick in some places. The tower was rebuilt into a prison after its military significance had become negligible in the 19th century. It operated as a prison until the early 20th century. The tower now houses the National Maritime Museum.

Great Coastal Gate viewed from the town

Passanger Port
Sea Centre
Great Coast Gate
Fat Margaret Tower
Margarethe`s Garden
Rannavärava
Rannamäe road
Tolli
Pikk
Lai
Uus
St. Olav`s Church
Oleviste
Suurtüki
Laboratooriumi
Pagari
Kotzebue
Vana-Kalamaja
Kesk-Kalamaja
Põhja road
Kopli
Rannamäe road
Reisijate
Railway Station
Towers Square
Kooli
City Theatre
Aida
Vaimu
Sulevimägi
Olevimägi
Brookus Square
Aia
Kanuti
Mere road
Kanut`s Garden
Gümnaasiumi
Transfiguration Church
Suur-Kloostri
Väike-Kloostri
Green Market
Vene
Bremen Passage
Nikolai Church
Snell Pond
Nunne
Dome Park
Puppet Theatre
Hobusepea
Börs passage
Pühavaimu
Munga
Great Guild Square
Holy Ghost Church
Peter Paul`s Church
Inseneri
Adventist Church
Rahukohtu
Toom-Rüütli
Church Square
Kiriku
Kohtu
Bishop`s Garden
Von Krahl Theatre
Rataskaevu
Voorimehe
Kinga
Mündi
Saiakang
Apteegi
Town Hall Square
Catherine`s passage
Müürivahe
Vana-Viru
Viru Square
Bastion Garden
The Long Leg
Dunkri
Town Hall
Raekoja
Old market place
The wheel well
The Dome Church
Toom-Kooli
Piiskopi
Rutu
Küllassepa
Old Market
Viru
Niguliste
Kuninga
The Long Leg
The Short Leg
Sauna
Viru Gate
Viru Gate Hill
Valli
Pärnu road
Tammsaare Park
Alexander Nevsky Cathedral
Palace Square
St. Nicholas Church
Vana-Posti
Väike-Karja
Governor`s Garden
Commandant`s Garden
Maiden Tower
Harju
Rüütli
Swedish St. Mikael`s Church
Suur-Karja
New Market
Drama Theatre
Estonia Theatre
Estonia road
Falgi road
Kiek in de Kök
Müürivahe
Rüütli
Komandandi
G. Otsa
Linda Hill
Toompea
Harju Gate Hill
Mayer`s Stairs
St. John`s Church
Deer`s Park
Vabaduse Square
Sakala
Sakala Centre
Iceland`s Square
Wismari
Old Town Studio
Kaarli road
Russian Drama Theatre
Kentmanni
Rävala road
Lembitu
Roosikrantsi
Pärnu road
Tatari
Charles`s Church

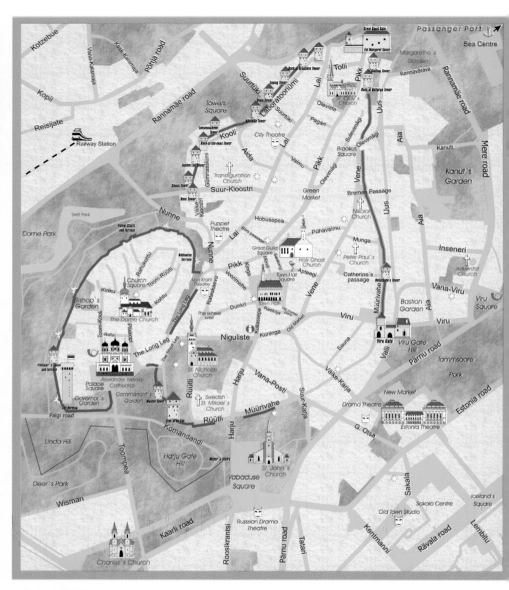

TALLINN

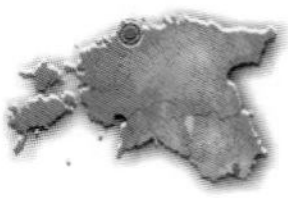

- Railway terminal
- Post office
- Theatre
- Museum
- Pharmacy
- Passanger port
- Church
- Sight
- Tourist information
- Town wall